MAGIC JOHNSON

★★★★★★★★★★★★★

LARRY BIRD

BY BRUCE WEBER

D1570333

AVON SUPERSTARS

AVON BOOKS
A division of
The Hearst Corporation
1790 Broadway
New York, New York 10019

First Avon Printing, February 1986

AVON TRADEMARK REG. U.S. PAT. OFF. AND IN
OTHER COUNTRIES, MARCA REGISTRADA, HECHO EN
U.S.A.

Printed in the U.S.A.

OP 10 9 8 7 6 5 4 3 2 1

Introduction
The Two and Only

Over the years, the NCAA championship has produced memorable basketball games, and personal match ups have highlighted previous tourney finals. But few match ups had excited fans across America like the 1979 NCAA Final. It was the match up everyone had waited all season to see: Larry Bird versus Magic Johnson. Bird, a senior at Indiana State, had virtually made the ISU program. Literally forgotten in even their home state, the Sycamores were considered only the fourth best team in Indiana. But Larry Bird and his awesome talent had been able to transform a group of no-names into a national title contender.

Earvin Johnson, Jr., known as Magic, had come to Michigan State with all the fanfare of a two-time high school all-American. And Magic turned his team, MSU, into a national power!

With this buildup, it was not surprising that more than 15,000 fans were shoehorned into the University of Utah's Special Events Center for the final game. Thousands more would like to have attended, but the Salt Lake City fire department was having none of it. They, like millions of others, would have to be content with watching it on television.

It became apparent rather early that the Michigan State group just had too much firepower. In addition to Magic Johnson, they had stars like Greg Kelser and Jay Vincent, while I S U had Bird, and little else to challenge the Michigan State quintet.

The final score was Michigan State 75, Indiana State 64. A convincing win for the men from Michigan. Yet, because Larry Bird was playing with an injured thumb, there would always be a question. Did that make a difference? Who would know?

But Bird was limited to 7 for 21 from the field, 19 points, and only 2 assists. All those numbers were far below his normal output. On the other side, Magic had 24 and Greg Kelser another 19 as the Spartans won the big one.

Larry Bird collapsed into a chair on the Indiana State bench, as Earvin (Magic) Johnson raced around the court hugging one teammate, slapping another, and carrying a third. This round went to Johnson.

But as Bird sat quietly on the sideline, he knew that their paths would cross again. And indeed, as we shall see, Larry Bird–Magic Johnson has become a major theme in the National Basketball Association championships. These two young men, the extroverted Johnson and the introverted Bird, had only played out the first show in an extended series.

1
Michigan Magic

Earvin Johnson, Jr.'s phenomenal success with the Lakers hardly came as a surprise to anyone in Lansing, Michigan.

Born on August 14, 1959, young Earvin and his six brothers and sisters grew up—thanks to the efforts of his parents, Earvin, Sr. and Christine—relatively free of problems. Earvin, the oldest, shared a room—and, for a long while, a bed—with his brother Larry. Brother Quincy completed the male trio. The four girls—Kim, Lily, and the twins, Evelyn and Yvonne—shared another bedroom.

The Johnson children were typical kids. They played hard, they fought hard, and they really loved one another. That was quite an achievement for their parents. Earvin, Sr., who wanted to do the best he could for his family, held two full-time jobs, which took up most of his 24-hour day. Eventually, Mrs. Johnson took a full-time job as well to help support the family.

Young Earvin saw the physical sacrifices his parents were making to help give the Johnson children as much as they could. "One day," he promised his mother, "I'm going to make it, and I'll take care of you." It was a promise he never forgot.

Earvin's parents had grown up in the South, his father in Mississippi and his mother in North Carolina. After their marriage, Earvin Sr. took a job with Fisher Body, the maker of General Motors auto bodies, in Lansing, where they raised all their children.

Earvin and Christine were deeply religious people, and Christine made sure that her children were involved in church activities. "All of the children were ushers at church or were in the choir," Mrs. Johnson remembers. "Earvin had lots of musical talent. I thought he had a future in music."

But Earvin was clearly in love with basketball.

Magic's legendary career began at a young age. Earvin gained a lifelong supporter at an early age, Dr. Charles Tucker. Tucker had plenty of basketball experience in college ball and even briefly in the pros. But by the time he was in his mid-twenties, his basketball career was behind him. After earning his doctorate, he took a job as a school psychologist in the Lansing public schools system. This career move was probably one of the best breaks young Earvin Johnson ever got.

By the time he started junior high school, people all over Lansing were hearing about the talented Johnson. And why not? The seventh grader was already 6 feet tall. He grew 4 more inches by eighth grade and another inch by ninth, and during that time his fame was growing just as fast.

Players from all over Lansing were heading to the west side, where Johnson played, to try their moves against the young hotshot. At that time Earvin developed an intense rivalry with one player in particular, Jay Vincent, with whom he went head-to-head throughout their junior high and high school careers. They would later become college teammates, and Jay would go on to become an NBA star himself with the Dallas Mavericks.

And then Dr. Tucker entered young Earvin's life. A psychologist in the Lansing schools, the older man helped Johnson channel his energies, mind, and goals. Their relationship started out with a chance meeting at Earvin's junior high school, developed during a one-on-one game, and continues to this day. Whenever

Earvin was troubled, Tucker was there to help.

Earvin wasn't thrilled about attending Everett High School. Most of his junior high friends had gone on to Sexton High. But the city of Lansing had to redistrict to meet desegregation rules, and that forced Earvin to go to Everett—where the basketball coach, Larry Fox, had previously cut Earvin's brother Larry from the team. Thanks to Earvin's basic level-headedness, and to some wise counseling by Tucker, however, he went all out to vindicate his brother.

Earvin moved right into the starting lineup as a sophomore. The coach could hardly have held him back; he was just too good. But it did create problems with some of his teammates, who didn't like taking a back seat to the newcomer—even one as talented as Johnson. Initially, coach George Fox had been unprepared to deal with Johnson's flamboyant style, but after a difficult start and with Tucker's help, the two learned to work together. Everyone benefited.

By mid-season, everyone in town was talking about Earvin Johnson, Jr. and the Everett High basketball team, the Vikings. Earvin, playing both center and forward, was doing it all. In one game alone, he tossed in 36 points, grabbed 18 rebounds, and dished out 16 assists. He was amazing.

The crowd gathered around Earvin's locker after that game, Vikings' supporters pumping his hand and congratulating him, and reporters asking all sorts of questions.

One of the writers, Fred Stabley, Jr., of the *Lansing State Journal,* was particularly impressed.

"I'd like to give you a nickname," Stabley said to the smiling youngster. "What about Magic?"

Earvin Johnson said, "Sure. Why not?"

And Magic it was. Outside of his family, few folks ever called him Earvin again. It was Magic this, and Magic that.

To the delight of Viking fans, he lived up to the nickname. During his sophomore year, the 6-foot, 5-inch Magic Man led the Vikings to a 22–2 record, losing only to Northeastern High of

Detroit and Fordson High of Dearborn. The latter defeat, in the state quarterfinals, really stung Johnson. The Vikings blew a 13-point lead in the final 8 minutes, including some missed one-and-one opportunities from the foul line during the closing moments by Magic.

Naturally, the experience upset him. But Tucker's steadying influence helped him keep his head on straight. He taught Earvin to control his emotions, which, in turn, helped him grow as a player and as a person.

While maintaining his grades and participating in numerous other school activities, including the newspaper, Magic worked hard to polish his game. He played daily—and everywhere—against all sorts of competition. He even spent countless hours at Michigan State, refining his skills by working out with college varsity players.

Despite Magic's summer practices and the coach's decision to move him to point guard, the next season turned into another disappointment when the Vikings lost their semifinal game in the state championship tournament after being ahead by 5 points at halftime.

The following season, Magic's senior year in high school, he once again led his team into the state tournament. In an opening round game, the Vikings crushed Eastern High, to whom they had lost during the season. They won because they stopped Eastern's star, Jay Vincent, who would become Magic's college teammate and then go on to a great career in the NBA with the Dallas Mavericks.

The Vikings breezed through the rest of the tournament until the final game, which they won in overtime. Magic finally had his championship. In the future there would be many more national championships on the college and pro levels. But that first one, with all the obstacles that had been overcome, was —well—magic!

2
The Spartan Life

Long before the last basketball swished through the hoop at the Michigan state high school tournament final, the name Magic Johnson had become a household word. And his talents caught the fancy of every major basketball coach in the nation. A great many of those coaches made their way to the yellow frame house on Middle Street to woo the talented son of Mr. and Mrs. Earvin Johnson, Sr.

At first, Magic was quite impressed with the attention. After a short time, however, it became overwhelming. Fortunately, he received plenty of support—from coach George Fox, from principal Frank Throop, and, of course, from Dr. Tucker. The final selection came down to the powerful, heavily supported program of Michigan, or Magic's own neighborhood school, Michigan State.

Magic was really impressed with the University of Michigan. But everyone in Lansing was begging him to stay home and lead the Michigan State Spartans. More important, Magic's dad was possibly the biggest State booster of all. Earvin, Sr. not only liked State but liked the idea of having his son playing in his hometown. Magic, however, was somewhat nervous about playing for State's tough coach, Jud Heathcote.

Eventually, after weighing the pros and cons of both schools, Magic selected State. Suddenly, Magic and his longtime rival, Jay Vincent, were united in the most impressive freshman group ever recruited in East Lansing. "I see an NCAA championship in Michigan State's future," Magic Johnson said. Only time would tell how accurate a fortune-teller he was.

The Johnson magic had an immediate impact on the MSU hoop program. From his first day at State, Earvin Johnson, Jr. was the most talked about man on campus.

Following a longstanding policy, Spartan basketball practice sessions were open to the public. But after just a few days, the practices began outdrawing the previous seasons' games. Coach Heathcote was, reluctantly, forced to change the policy. With such large crowds on hand he simply could not get enough teaching done. Nevertheless, the press, which remained eligible for admittance, made up a decent crowd by itself. Consequently, Magic and his teammates were examined under a media microscope long before they played their first regular-season game.

By now, Michigan State fans were in a frenzy, despite the previous season's record of 10-17. With veteran forward Greg Kelser, a sharpshooter and a strong rebounder in the lineup, and the presence of rookies Johnson and Vincent, big things were expected.

By the time MSU opened its season against Central Michigan, a ticket to Jenison Field House was the hottest item in Lansing. Although Magic had what he considered a disappointing start, Vincent's 25 points led the Spartans to victory.

It didn't take long, however, for Magic to find the groove, and the ever-present smile on his shining face grew broader as Spartan victories piled up. Years of training in the gym with Michigan Staters during his high school days had finally paid off: He quickly learned how a college team differed from a team of high schoolers. College players, Magic already knew, were smarter, quicker, bigger, stronger, and, most of all, better than the players he had faced at Everett.

Led by Johnson, the Spartans won as never before. The team went 25–5, winning their first Big 10 championship in 19 years. In fact, it marked the first time ever that a Michigan State team won more than 20 games. It seemed that everyone on campus was smiling as broadly as Magic Johnson. (Only a loss to top-ranked Kentucky, in the NCAA Mideast Regional final, spoiled the year—but not by much!)

But the smiles of the fans turned to frowns of concern immediately after the season was over. Rumors began to fly fast and furiously. "Will Magic turn pro?" was the most talked-about question in town.

In the end, he decided to stay. Lansing heaved a sigh of relief that could be felt throughout the Big 10, the conference that State is a part of. Even gruff Jud Heathcote was seen grinning broadly.

That summer, instead of showing up at an NBA training camp, Magic joined a couple of world tours, which enabled him to play with a variety of college stars, including his once-and-future rival, Larry Bird. Magic loved the experience, and he never regretted his decision to pass up the pros at that time.

The well-traveled Magic returned to Michigan State in the fall, ready to face the most intense pressure he'd ever known. Every expert had picked Michigan State to be one of the Top Ten teams in the country, and despite the fact that he had played only one year of college ball, Earvin Johnson was the cover boy for *Sports Illustrated*'s basketball preview issue.

Unfortunately, press notices and reality don't always mesh. The Spartans got off to a dismal start in Magic's sophomore year. Eight games into the Big 10 season, everyone's conference favorites found themselves 4–4. The press heaped the heat on the Magic Man, who had never been the target of such criticism before. But a tough team meeting with coach Heathcote, a couple of lineup changes, and a rededication by the team helped turn things around.

By season's end, the Spartans had run off nine straight league wins (before one season-ending loss). They had caught up with everyone, tied for the Big 10 title—and thus won a bid to the NCAA tournament.

The winner of the tournament is crowned the king of college basketball. That was the team's target. The memory of their loss to Kentucky the previous year was still fresh in their minds. Given an opportunity to do what they thought they could do—win a national championship—they vowed to make the most of it.

State had an excellent starting five, but bench strength was a question. In addition, Jay Vincent had suffered a stress fracture of his foot in the opening tourney game.

But, in quick order, Lamar fell, then Louisiana State. Michigan State was on fire during their meeting with Notre Dame, and they bombed the Fighting Irish by 12 points. They had won the regional, which they had lost the previous year, and had earned a trip to the Final Four.

Penn—the tournament's Cinderella team—was Michigan State's semifinal opponent. Heathcote prepared the Spartans well, taking them to Salt Lake City, site of the Final Four, two days early. The clock struck midnight for Cinderella, and Penn never had a chance. Johnson and Kelser hooked up on alley-oop stuffs, Magic worked his, well, magic, and the Spartans blew out to an unbelievable 33-point halftime lead. They won the semifinal game by 34 points, the biggest rout in Final Four history.

Meanwhile, in the other semifinal, top-ranked Indiana State, led by Larry Bird, had upended second-ranked DePaul, who had been led by Mark Aguire, by a single point. This set up the Dream Final between Magic and Bird.

MSU's match up zone clipped Bird's wings as he was able to sink only 7 for 21 from the field—and the Spartans easily tucked the 1979 national championship away.

Magic was the man of the hour. He hit on 8 of 15 from the floor, 8 of 10 from the foul line (for a 24-point total), grabbed 7 rebounds, and dished off 5 assists. (About the only thing he didn't do was pull rabbits out of his hat.) The MVP voting wasn't even close; it was Magic in a landslide.

The entire city of Lansing went mad. Their hometown hero, who had won an MVP title and a state high school championship only 2 years earlier, had capped it with a repeat performance on the college level.

Mission accomplished, Magic again had to wrestle with the decision to stay at State or enter the NBA draft and begin his professional career.

There were plenty of reasons to stay: his education, another national crown, the Olympics, campus life. Magic, though, also relished the challenge of playing pro ball.

During the weeks to come, Magic, his advisers, and his attorneys devoted countless hours to the decision: stay or go. Both his father and Dr. Tucker were leaning toward the pros. As the dollars mounted—up toward half a million—Magic's resistance wore down. He wanted very much to stay in college, but the lure of the NBA was magnetizing.

The top pick in the NBA draft that year belonged to the Los Angeles Lakers. The opportunity to play with Kareem, the best center and possibly the best player in the history of the game, was, no doubt, an important consideration. But also the opportunity to gain financial security for himself and his parents, who had worked so hard for their family, would prove a strong pull.

3
Welcome to Tinseltown

Up until the final moments before the press conference to announce his signing, Christine Johnson begged her son to remain in college.

"I've got to try it," Magic told his mom. He felt he had done it all in high school and college, and he was now searching for a new and lucrative challenge.

"Just promise me that you'll go to school during the off-season," his mother asked, resigned to the fact that the NBA would be Magic's new home.

"You've got it, Mom," said Earvin, Jr. To this day, he has faithfully kept that promise.

A week later, against a backdrop of popping flashbulbs and a crush of newsmen, the Lakers introduced their upcoming first-round draft choice. Johnson's famed smile and bubbling enthusiasm were clearly in evidence. A big-city press conference can prove a stern challenge for someone as young as Magic Johnson, but he parried every tough question with a confident answer.

Confidence and enthusiasm—those had become Magic's stock in trade. Still, there were critics who doubted his ability to carry his exuberant, upbeat style into the NBA. But Magic never doubted his ability to step in and play a major role with the Lakers.

In addition to playing in quite a few charity all-star games around the country, Magic joined the Lakers' rookie team for a game in the Southern California Rookie League. Was L.A. geared up for the arrival of the Magic One? You know it. Instead of the typical crowd of 400 or 500, nearly 5,000 fans showed up at Cal State L.A. for the game. And a few thousand more were turned away. Tinseltown, otherwise known as Los Angeles, was ready for Magic and his bag of tricks.

So, apparently, were the Lakers. "At first, we couldn't believe him," recalls teammate Jamaal Wilkes. "He was *so* enthusiastic. We weren't sure it was genuine. But it was. That's him. That's Magic."

There were a few initial adjustments to make, however, by both Magic and his new teammates. Guard Norm Nixon, who had controlled the Laker offense, had to yield some of his ball-handling chores to Magic, who impressed everyone with his no-look passes. "We were still bumping into each other by mid-season," remembers Nixon. "But it sure wasn't dull."

When opening night rolled around on October 12, 1979, the Forum was packed—more than 17,000 people showed up. The Lakers had plenty of stars, but almost everyone was there to see the new kid on the block. During the previous season, attendance at a Lakers' game had only averaged about 12,000, so Magic's impact was felt immediately.

Magic fit in right away, hitting Kareem Abdul-Jabbar with beautiful lob passes all night. But as the clock wound down, it was up to Kareem to do his thing, and his 18-foot skyhook gave the Lakers a 103–102 win and, in newspapers throughout the country, fans were greeted the next morning by a photo of twenty-year-old rookie Johnson, with a smile as wide as the Mississippi, in the loving embrace of his veteran center, Abdul-Jabbar.

It didn't take long for the rest of the NBA to find out that this rookie—despite only 2 years of college experience—was indeed ready for the pros. The Lakers, off a decent 47–35 season, weren't expected to challenge Seattle for the Western Conference title. But the youngster's talent, drive, and enthusiasm quickly began to affect his teammates—and their rivals.

Talk about confidence—in one game, only a month into the season, Magic tossed in 31 points in addition to playing his usual floor game. Later, in response to a reporter's question after the game, he said, "When we've got it going and the fast break is flowing, I suppose it looks like I can perform magic on the court. On some nights, I think I can do anything."

Kareem Abdul-Jabbar was totally impressed. "Magic does so many unbelievable things on the court that you work harder to make his plays pay off. It's great to play with him."

Magic felt the same way about Kareem, whom he always called "Big Fella." He credited Abdul-Jabbar with smoothing the way during his first season, teaching him on the court and guiding him off it. After all, Magic reasoned, Kareem had once been the most talked-about rookie in the league and understood the pressures of being in that position.

A sprained knee sidelined Magic for a couple of weeks early in the season, but even that couldn't stop him.

Three months after the action-packed opener, Magic became the first rookie in 11 years to start in the All-Star game.

Meanwhile, the Lakers were rolling. A solid victory over defending western champ Seattle vaulted the team into first place. And they held on for the rest of the season, ending with a 95–93 victory over the Warriors in Oakland. Appropriately, the winning basket was scored off a patented no-look pass from Magic Johnson.

Johnson's season numbers were impressive. He hit on 503 of 949 field-goal attempts, giving him a .530 percentage. No Laker rookie had ever performed better. He dished off 563 assists, another team mark for rookies. He averaged 18.0 points per game and pulled down 7.7 rebounds per contest, second best ever for an NBA guard. The awards followed quickly—including a unanimous vote to the league's All-Rookie Team and a second place finish, behind Larry Bird, in the voting for the Rookie of the Year prize.

For those who believe that the NBA season is merely a warm-up for the play-offs, the real season still lay ahead. By winning the Pacific title, the Lakers drew the Phoenix Suns in the opening round of the play-offs. The Suns fell in 5 games.

Next they met the defending conference champion, the Seattle SuperSonics. Again it took only 5 games for the Lakers to end the Seattle season.

The finals matched L.A. against the powerful Philadelphia 76ers, who were led by the incomparable Dr. J—Julius Erving. The Lakers owned the home-court advantage, but that was quickly lost when L.A. split the first 2 games at home. Needing a win to recover the edge, the Lakers pulled it off by splitting in Philly.

With 2 wins each, the series had become a best-of-three affair. Magic and his teammates returned to L.A., knowing what they had to do.

Led by Kareem Abdul-Jabbar, the Lakers took game 5. Kareem was incredible. At the end of the third period, he sprained his left ankle so badly that he had to leave the floor and have it heavily wrapped. Still he returned in the final period to clinch the victory by tossing in 14 of his game-high 40 points.

Kareem's injury was so bad, however, that he couldn't make the trip to Philadelphia for game 6. Everyone thought his absence would cause L.A. to lose the game, and the Lakers simply hoped they could get the Big Fella ready for game 7, back in L.A. But "everyone" hadn't counted on Magic Johnson. And a startling move by the coach—moving Magic from point guard to center!

Actually, Magic did a little more than that. He played center (both high and low post), point guard, shooting guard, small forward, and power forward. It was quite possibly the most amazing performance ever in a championship game.

Without Jabbar, L.A. wasn't even expected to be in the hunt, but throughout the game the Sixers couldn't shake them. By halftime, when the score was tied at 60–60, the fans in the Spectrum (Philly's arena) and in front of TV sets across the nation knew something special was happening.

L.A. scored the first 14 points of the third quarter, and, while they had to turn back a couple of rallies which were led by Julius Erving, they remained on top all the way.

The Magic Man had been merely incredible. In 47 minutes at all five positions, he tossed in 42 points (on 14 of 23 from the field and 14 of 14 from the foul line). He had 15 rebounds, 7 assists, 3 steals, and even blocked a shot. He was virtually a one-man wrecking crew in the 123–107 victory—though Wilkes's 37 points (including 25 in the second half) really helped.

In the glow of the winning locker room, Magic, smiling more broadly than ever, gave all the credit to his absent teammate, Kareem. "The Big Fella brought us here," he gushed. "Without him, we'd never have been here. We won it for him—and us!"

Evidently, the MVP voters thought a little more of Magic than he did of himself. Capping an incredible rookie season, he won a narrow one-vote victory over Kareem for the play-off MVP award.

It had been quite a ride from the press conference in East Lansing to the wild locker-room celebration in Philadelphia. There were plenty of hugs and even more smiles. But difficult times were on the horizon.

4
When the Going
Gets Tough . . .

When the Lakers' plane landed back home in Los Angeles, Kareem Abdul-Jabbar was there to greet his teammates.

The Big Fella strode straight up to the beaming Magic Johnson and embraced him. "Welcome home, hero," said Kareem.

"It doesn't get any better than this," Magic thought. Even the totally optimistic Johnson could hardly believe the great good fortune he had enjoyed during the previous 14 months: an NCAA championship and an MVP award, a mega-bucks contract with a great pro club, an NBA title, another MVP trophy, and national acclaim for one of the most spectacular performances ever seen on a basketball court.

"What can you possibly do now?" asked one reporter after another.

To which Magic Johnson confidently replied, "Another title next year." And he really meant it.

But when the 1980–81 season rolled around, Earvin Johnson, Jr. learned a few of the reasons why no NBA team had won back-to-back championships in nearly two decades. Athletes, he found out, are horribly fragile instruments. And it's only a fine line that separates the very good teams from the exceptional ones.

Early in the season, Magic collided with Dallas big man Tom LaGarde. A hefty 7-footer, LaGarde banged into Magic's left knee. Johnson, who had never been seriously hurt before, was concerned.

Magic, however, kept playing. He was going great. He was up among the league leaders in scoring, and he was number one in both steals and assists. The team was 15–5, rolling along atop the Pacific Division.

Magic's joy was short-lived, however. Early in the second quarter of a game against Kansas City, he tried to cut past his man. He went one way, his left knee went the other way, and the snapping sound and the incredible pain in his knee told him something was dreadfully wrong. It would require an operation.

The collapse of Magic's knee led to the collapse of the Lakers, too. They went into an immediate tailspin, losing 5 of their next 8 games. Although they improved somewhat as they grew used to Magic's absence and the shock of their sudden loss lessened, they still weren't the same team. "We miss him as much off the court as we do on it," said coach Paul Westhead.

The rehabilitation of Johnson's knee was a slow process—and an extremely difficult one. It began the day after the operation and became more complex every day. Once the cast was off, Magic began showing up at the Lakers' home court, the Forum, for their games, but that just made him more anxious than ever to return to the court. Accordingly, he went back to Lansing for a few days and spent every morning running with Dr. Tucker, who was impressed by Magic's hard work.

The hard work paid off. By early February, 10 weeks after the injury, Magic was back at practice. But he wasn't quite ready to return to the NBA wars. Meanwhile, the Lakers, who had suffered for a while, were beginning to play better. Magic's workouts became harder and harder.

Finally, on February 27, when everyone was convinced that Magic was fit to play again, he returned to the Laker lineup. It had been nearly 3½ months of frustration, but the lessons Magic had learned—of patience and of his own vulnerability—were almost worth it.

The Lakers, off their 15–5 start with Johnson, had won 28 of 45 while he was away. During the last 6 weeks of the season, they won 11 of the last 18. Magic led the NBA with 3.43 steals per game (a total of 127). And he finished with 21.6 points per game in his 37 outings, his best scoring year ever. He hit on 53.1 percent of his field goals and 76 percent of his free throws.

The problem was that the team had never really succeeded in putting it all together. During Magic's absence, Westhead constantly juggled the lineup. This caused many of the players to become disgruntled, and the team was in an ongoing state of confusion. And if the basketball world needed any proof of that, it came quickly. The first round of the play-offs were a best-two-of-three affair. L.A. drew the mediocre Houston Rockets. The Rockets were led by the great Moses Malone, but his supporting cast was undistinguished.

It was surprising, although hardly shocking, that Houston won their home play-off game. Combined with a Los Angeles victory in game 1, that set up a winner-take-all game 3 back in the Forum.

That game was a shocker. Houston led most of the way, but with 5 seconds to go, the Lakers had a chance to win. The ball went to Magic for the game-winning shot. He arced a jumper toward the hoop, but Moses Malone leaped up and swatted the ball away. When the final second blinked off the clock, the Rockets had won, 89–86, and once again, the defending NBA champions had failed to defend.

"The trouble is, we became a team of individuals this season," Magic said. "We had some guys who became more interested in 'I' than 'we.' "

Even though the Lakers had lost, Magic Johnson was about to gain a personal victory from Lakers owner Dr. Jerry Buss. Buss was concerned with the NBA's new free-agent rules, which allow a player to go to the highest bidder after his contract expires.

"The thought of not having Magic with the Lakers is unthinkable," Buss said. "He's a fantastic player and a great person. I want to keep him in Los Angeles forever."

The only way Buss could conceive of accomplishing this feat was through a contract extension that surpassed all other contract extensions in the history of professional sports.

It wasn't the biggest contract in terms of dollars per year, but the number of years under contract set the sports world buzzing. Magic was granted an additional *25 years* at one million dollars per. "I expect another ten years in uniform," Buss said, "then he'll work for me for the duration of the contract. He could coach, he could run the team, he could even run the business."

Consequently, when the 1981–82 season started, there was even more pressure on Magic. The play-off failure of the previous season, in addition to the "lifetime" contract, created a tension that had never existed before. And things were about to get worse.

Coach Paul Westhead became more determined than ever to mold the Lakers his way. He required far more set plays on offense, which would greatly inhibit Johnson's freewheeling style, which had brought the Lakers the NBA championship. It didn't sit well with many of the players. And the most unhappy of the complainers was Magic Johnson.

As Magic saw it, Westhead's structured offense wasn't going to help the Lakers. In fact, he believed that it would inhibit their joy on the court and hurt their won-lost record, as well. Unlike his other teammates, who complained in private or silently, Magic was outspoken. Finally, about a month into the season, he laid out an ultimatum for his boss, Jerry Buss. It's either Paul or me, Johnson said—more or less. If he stays, I want to be traded.

The results were predictable. Within hours, Westhead was no longer coach. Laker fans blamed Magic for playing a major role in Westhead's departure, and they were angry. The next time Magic suited up at the Forum, he was roundly booed; his popularity with the fans had fallen from its lofty peak.

Fortunately, neither Magic's play nor the team's was adversely affected. In fact, under Westhead's successor Pat Riley (a former Lakers player and broadcaster before joining Westhead on the bench as an assistant coach), both the Lakers and Magic flourished. The Lakers, 7-4 (not that bad) under Westhead, won 17 of their next 20 games. At 24-7, they led second-place Seattle by 5 games.

Magic enjoyed one of his best all-around seasons, becoming only the third player in history to record more than 700 points (he had 1,447), 700 rebounds (he had 751), and 700 assists (743) in one season. It was a sparkling performance that got the Lakers flying into the play-offs.

He also changed the way NBA teams filled the point-guard position forever. It was simply amazing that a 6-9 guard could lead the league in steals (2.67 that season) for 2 straight years, while also finishing second in assists (9.5 per game). But when a point guard also sets a record with 13 offensive rebounds in one game, then opposition has to give serious thought to whom they assign to guard that player. He's much too quick for players his own size, all of whom play the forward position, and he's too tall for the smaller guards, who are usually 5 inches shorter than he is.

When the play-offs began, Magic and his teammates really caught fire. They quickly disposed of both Phoenix and Midwest champion San Antonio in 4 straight games each, the first time any team had swept two opponents back to back. And when they defeated the 76ers in the opening game of the finals, they became the first team ever to win 9 straight play-off contests.

The victory at Philly was made all the more remarkable by the fact that the Lakers had not played in 12 days and should have been rusty. While L.A. was sweeping its western opponents, the Eastern teams were fighting it out every night. The Boston-Philly Eastern final had gone the full 7 games, before the Sixers prevailed, so Philadelphia was razor sharp.

Philadelphia came back, though, and took game 2. It was the Lakers' first loss in nearly 7 weeks!

Back in L.A., Magic was assigned the task of keeping 76er superstar, Julius ("Dr. J") Erving, off the boards. Dr. J had grabbed an impressive 23 rebounds in the first 2 games of the series, but with Magic working hard to box him off the boards, Erving was limited to only 3 rebounds in game 3. Magic felt good, though he realized that few fans would ever figure out why, since keeping your man off the boards doesn't show up in a statistic sheet. More important, the Lakers won game 3 easily. And they took game 4 by 10, setting up a possible clincher back in Philly.

But the 76ers wouldn't cooperate, and it wasn't even close. L.A. virtually disappeared during the second half. From midway through the third quarter to the final buzzer, Philadelphia outscored Los Angeles 61–30! The Sixers won by 33 points, and Magic was hurting: His knuckles, sore going into the game, were further banged up on a steal attempt in the first quarter.

Both teams were ready to go all out in game 6. But L.A. came out blazing and raced to a 9–0 lead. It wasn't a blow-out, but Philly never did gain the lead, despite coming close in the third quarter. Dr. J even had a chance to tie the score once, but Bob McAdoo swatted the shot away. The Lakers then cruised to a fairly easy 114–104 victory.

The locker room was a scene right out of Hollywood. The noise level was in the loud zone, with lots of high-fives, embraces, and loud whoops. Coach Riley, who'd been just an assistant coach when the year started, gave Magic a big hug and said quietly, "Thanks."

It was a night of 13's—but not unlucky ones—for Magic. He had 13 points, 13 assists, and 13 rebounds in the finale. He also received his second play-off MVP award in 3 years, which coincided with the Lakers' second title in 3 seasons. Could they break the jinx and turn in a repeat performance the following year? Only time would tell.

5

The Road to Victory

The championship, L.A.'s second in 3 years with Abdul-Jabbar on the inside and Magic on the outside, helped crown Earvin Johnson, Jr. as the king of Los Angeles. Laker fans loved having the NBA title in town again and hoped at last to see the repeat jinx, which began in 1969, finally broken.

More than that, however, they took Magic Johnson to their hearts. And why not? Magic was the most exciting thing to happen to Los Angeles since Al Jolson promised, "You ain't seen nothin' yet" in the first talking movie, more than 50 years earlier.

Magic reveled in his great fame and popularity. It propelled him into the '82–'83 season, which would become his first on the All-NBA first team. He led the league in assists with 10.5 per game, the only player in the league to average more than 10. And with 683 rebounds, he missed the magic 700 mark by only 17 boards. Had he grabbed those 17 (and he missed three games along the way), he'd have become only the third player in league history to go over 700 in points, assists, and rebounds in one season. The other two? Oscar Robertson and Wilt Chamberlain. Not bad company: two of the greatest players in the history of the game.

Still, he was the leading rebounder among NBA guards (8.6 per game) and was the Lakers' top foul shooter (80.0%). His 829 assists set a new Laker team record, which had been held by former super-star Jerry West, now the team's general manager.

Magic became the master of the "triple-double." When a player gets 10 or more points, rebounds, or assists, they're called double figures. When a player gets doubles in all three categories, it's called a triple-double. During the '82–'83 season, Magic, with 16 triple-doubles, was the clear league-leader. He also had 35 other games in which he had a double-double. That shows great all-around ability and desire.

The Golden State Warriors knew all about Magic's versatility. On April 8, in the game that clinched the Pacific Division title, Magic dished off 12 assists in the first half, setting a Forum record, then hit 9 straight shots in the third quarter, setting a team record. Overall, he finished with 36 points—his season high—13 rebounds, and 14 assists.

Critics were quick to point to his decreased scoring average (16.3, nearly 5 points under his best year and his lowest as a pro). But E. J. seemed to be getting more of a kick out of seeing teammates score off his passes. Against the Atlanta Hawks on January 15, for example, Magic scored his career high of 21 assists and a season high of 17 rebounds, but scored only 13 points.

Magic is, very simply, an unselfish player who cares more about team victories than personal point totals.

In the opening round of the 1983 playoffs against Portland, Kareem was scoring like a kid. First it was 32 points, then 37, then 30, then 34, until he hit a slump—only 21. Magic shared rebounding honors in the first game (18) and led in assists in 4 of the 5 series (with a one-game high of 18!) The Blazers won only once, as the Lakers breezed through a 4–1 series victory.

The San Antonio Spurs, led by Mike Mitchell and the high-scoring "Ice Man," George Gervin, were next. This match up was a little tougher. The Spurs stunned the Lakers by winning twice in L.A. But L.A. won three times in Texas. (So much for the home-court advantage!)

Kareem cooled off to a 26.3 ppg average (down from 30.8 in the series against the Blazers). But Magic averaged 17.5 points, 10.5 rebounds, and 14 assists—a triple-double average—for the six-game series. Magic was the leading scorer twice, the leading rebounder five times, and the assist leader five times.

The Lakers had gained the right to battle a fired-up 76er team and try for back-to-back championships.

The 76ers, led by Moses Malone (whom Philadelphia had obtained in a trade with Houston), the phenomenal Dr. J, and the sharp-shooting Andrew Toney, shocked the Lakers and totally wiped them out. Moses was awesome as he tossed in 25.8 points and grabbed 18 rebounds per game. The Lakers had been swept 4-0, once again.

Magic headed back to Lansing for the summer and back to Michigan State, where, as he'd promised his mom he'd do, he was still taking off-season courses in telecommunications. He went back to his softball team, back to his roots and his friends. The better to forget the Philadelphia 76ers.

The off-season has always been one of Magic's favorite times. The man loves his game, but he also loves his off-the-court activities. He devotes a great deal of time to charity, including helping to raise funds to fight the disease Sickle Cell Anemia; the Special Olympics, which provides an athletic experience for handicapped people; and the Landon Turner Foundation, which was founded when Indiana University basketball star Landon Turner was severely injured in an auto accident. Magic also established a program in Lansing called "Action Reading," which aids local students with reading problems. Although Magic has achieved great success, he's always happy to share the fruits of his success with others.

By the time he returned to L.A. for the 1983–84 season, the play-off disaster was behind him. He was fired up again and ready to go. The result was his best season to date.

Despite a dislocated finger, which kept him out of fifteen regular-season games, he managed to set a new Laker assist record while leading the league with 875 assists, a 13.2 per game average. He also averaged 2.24 steals per game, fifth best in the league.

Breaking records became routine for Magic. But more important his shooting improved. Year in and year out, he had been becoming a better outside shooter. As he had every season, he improved his field-goal percentage, this time bringing it to 56.5 percent, placing him tops among the league's starting guards. And in the triple-double department, he added another 12 games to his record, accompanied by a total of 43 double-doubles.

His efforts earned him a berth on the All-NBA first team for the second straight year. On *The Sporting News*'s All-NBA team, which is chosen by the players, Magic was the leading vote-getter.

The Lakers came through the season in fine shape, too, with a six-game edge over second-place Portland in the Pacific Division race. They carried their 54–28 record into the play-offs, with the objective of erasing the 4–0 blowout of the previous season.

The Kansas City Kings went down in three straight. Magic scored 26 points and 11 assists in game 1 and a triple-double (17 points, 10 rebounds, 13 assists) in game 3. His 35 assists marked the second-highest total ever for a three-game series.

The Dallas Mavericks were next. L.A. opened with an incredible 134–91 victory, won game 2, lost game 3 in Dallas 125–115, took an overtimer in game 4, and then romped again in L.A., 115–99, to cap a 4–1 victory in the best-of-seven series. Shooting guard Mike McGee had a super series, while Magic just did his everyday thing. He had 27 points to pace the Lakers in game 2 and a triple-double (14 points, 11 rebounds, 16 assists) in game 4. In all, he dished off 67 assists in the five games, again the second-highest total ever in a five-game series.

The Western finals, against Phoenix, were just a bit more competitive. Still, the Lakers dominated, taking easy victories in games 1 and 2 at home, winning each by 16 points. In game 3 a 135–127 overtime victory by the Suns in Phoenix added to the drama. But L.A. came back to win game 4 in Phoenix, 126–115, and take a 3–1 lead. Phoenix surprised the Lakers in L.A., 126–121, in game 5. But the Lakers ended it with a second road victory, 99–97, in game 6.

Magic was incredible in the second game, tossing off a league play-off record 24 assists. As a result, seven other Lakers scored in double figures. Another Magic triple-double (16 points, 11 rebounds, 13 assists) keyed the victory in the final game, and he totaled 67 assists for the six-game series.

The championship series against the Boston Celtics was exciting, exhausting, and, to students of basketball history, predictable. The league title had been up for grabs between the Lakers and Celtics seven times, including 1984, and each time, the Celtics had won. The Celtics were ready to add to the string.

It didn't start out that way, however. After a long cross-country trip, the Lakers, led by 32 Kareem Abdul-Jabbar points, surprised Boston, 115–109. Then, just when it looked as though L.A. would sweep a pair in the ancient Boston Garden, the Celts rallied to tie the score and win 124–121 in overtime. Magic scored 27 points in this one, trailing teammate James Worthy's 29. But it wasn't enough.

Still, the Lakers were returning home even, with the home-court advantage now leaning their way. The lean became an all-out tilt in game 3. Magic was incredible. He dished off 21 assists (a final-round record) and scored 14 points while grabbing 11 rebounds, giving him yet another amazing triple-double. The Lakers rolled, really rolled, 137–104.

The Lakers had Boston down again in game 4, before Larry Bird (29 points, 21 rebounds) helped the Celts into another overtime. Result: Boston 129, L.A. 125. Kareem's 32 points, Worthy's 30, and another triple-double by Magic (20 points, 11 boards, 17 assists) were wasted.

When the teams split games 5 and 6, each winning at home, the scene was set for a deciding game 7—at Boston, where the Celts had never lost a deciding game.

They didn't lose this one, either. Though the Celtics hit fewer than 40 percent of their shots, Boston won the battle of the back-boards, 52–33, and outscored the Lakers from the foul line at 43–18. The Celts' 111–102 victory sewed up their fifteenth title and maintained the Boston Garden mystique.

The thought of the Celtics' victory carried the Lakers through the season and the early-round play-off games in 1985. The chance to redeem themselves, to finally break through the Boston jinx, drove L.A. to three preliminary series wins, during which they lost only 2 games.

And more than any other Laker, Magic felt the need to redeem himself for the way he had thrown away last year's championship. And there were questions about how long Kareem could continue to play at the high level which he'd sustained over the years. The Lakers wanted to win now and reverse the humiliation of last year's defeat.

Game 1, though, gave new meaning to the word humiliation. It will forever be known as the "Memorial Day Massacre" or the "Boston Blowout." Boston shot better than 60 percent from the field, with Scott Wedman hitting 11 of 11. The Celts jumped out to a 47–25 lead, extended it to 63–34, and went on to win 148–114, the second-worst beating ever administered in an NBA final-round game.

"Not in my wildest dreams, or anybody's else's," said Magic, "did we think this would happen. We just got an old-fashioned whipping." Teammate Mike McGee put it even better, "Somebody told me this could have been a blessing in disguise. Well it certainly was well disguised."

Miraculously, L.A. bounced back in game 2. And it was the "old man," Kareem, who did it. He lectured his teammates before the game and then taught Boston a lesson on the floor. He had 30 points, 17 rebounds, and 8 assists, most of which set up teammate Michael Cooper. The most incredible statistic was that Boston had only three offensive rebounds. The Celtics, who thrive on the second and third try, had only three chances!

L.A.'s victory in game 3 at the Forum brought back memories of game 1, although Boston led after 17 minutes, 48–38. But then the Celtics seemed to go to sleep as L.A. came on. At one point, the Lakers outscored Boston, 60–32, and the final score was L.A. 136, Boston 111. Kareem became the all-time leading play-off scorer with a total of 4,458 (topping ex-Laker Jerry West's previous high of 4,457 points).

With two straight wins behind them, the Lakers felt great about game 4 in L.A. But the heroics of Larry Bird and what might be called a defensive goof by Magic enabled the Celts to tie it up. The lead had seesawed back and forth. Thanks to a run of 7 points by Bird and a couple of long jumpers by Danny Ainge, the teams came to the final seconds tied at 105.

The Celtics had the ball. As anyone who has ever seen the team play knows, Larry Bird takes the big shots for Boston, and that's exactly what the Lakers figured on. When Larry got the ball, Magic slid over from his man, Dennis Johnson, to double-team the blond bomber. But it was a mistake. Bird tossed the ball to D.J., who canned a 21-footer at the buzzer for the victory.

Why did Magic leave D.J. to cover Bird? "Larry has beaten us so much," said Magic of his longtime rival, "we'd prefer someone else take a chance on beating us. But Dennis knocked it down. I didn't think about it—until the shot went in the basket. That's when it hit me. We lost!"

The Lakers were now more determined than ever to put it all together. Game 5 of any series which is tied is usually the most crucial, because the winner takes a 3–2 lead and has two chances to sew it up. It was therefore essential for L.A. to win this one at home, in order to avoid going back to Boston for games 6 and 7 and having to win both.

Kareem and Magic did it all. Abdul-Jabbar had 36 points, 7 rebounds, 7 assists, and 3 blocks. Magic was equally incredible. He had 26 points and 17 assists, and he played like a demon all night. L.A. opened a 17-point lead, then held off Boston rushes

29

through the final period.

"We had to win this one," said Magic afterward. "It was getting where people were saying we can't win the big ones. Well, we showed them. We won it. We can win it all. We just have to put our minds to it."

Boston had, however, never lost the deciding game of a playoff final on its home court. In addition, L.A. and Boston had met eight times in the championship series. Boston had won every time.

Until this time. The score was tied 55-55 at the half, then the Lakers spurted ahead 73-63 early in the third period. That did it. Kareem had another brilliant night (29 points, 7 rebounds), and Magic recorded yet another triple-double (14 points, 10 boards, 11 assists). In addition to brilliant performances by Kareem and Magic, young James Worthy tossed in 28 points, and the Boston jinx was broken. Kareem took the MVP trophy—it was unanimous—but every Laker had contributed to the victory.

Coach Pat Riley was absolutely ecstatic. "The skeletons are out of the closet now," he said. "We passed the ultimate test. We won in Boston." Bostonians consider their city to be the cradle of the Revolutionary War and the home of basketball champions. *Fifteen* world-championship banners hang from the rafters of Boston Garden as a reminder of that fact to everyone.

Magic, exhausted, sat back in the Lakers' locker room, the ever-present smile broader, if possible, than ever. He gazed up and saw their last championship trophy, the trophy that had eluded the Lakers in two previous attempts.

"It was a long year, a very long year. Ever since they beat us here last year, we've waited for this chance. They said we couldn't win here. But we did it by outworking them, outhustling them, getting every loose ball—which we should have done last year. But no matter. We've done it now, and we've done it for all the Laker teams of the past that were frustrated here. This," he said slowly, "this is what you live for."

The sweet taste of victory at the 1979 NCAA championship.
(UPI/Bettmann Newsphotos)

Magic Johnson driving the court.

(John McDonough/Focus on Sports, Inc.)

The Magic Man against the Bird Man.

(Andrew D. Bernstein/Focus on Sports, Inc.)

Not every game is a victory.

(Jerry Wachter/Focus on Sports, Inc.)

Bird scores in Game 4 of the 1984 NBA finals.

(Andrew D. Bernstein/Focus on Sports, Inc.)

Magic passes the ball away from Bird.

(Focus on Sports, Inc.)

Magic, surrounded by fans, at his summer basketball camp.
(Andrew D. Bernstein/Focus on Sports, Inc.)

Coach Pat Riley and Magic Johnson meet the press.
(Richard Pilling/Focus on Sports, Inc.)

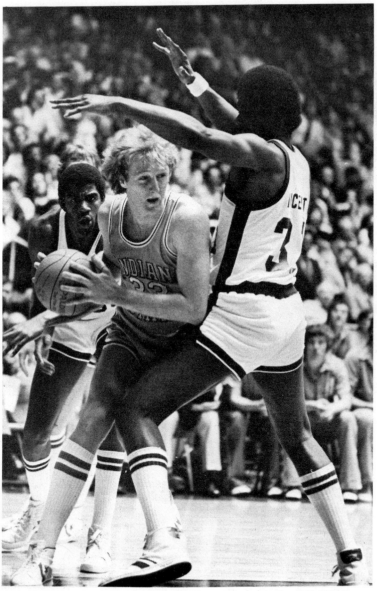

Larry Bird guarded by Jay Vincent and Magic Johnson at the 1979 NCAA championship. (UPI/Bettmann Newsphotos)

Larry Bird driving to the hoop.

(Focus on Sports, Inc.)

Larry Bird soars above everyone.

(Focus on Sports, Inc.)

Magic flashes his famous victory smile.

(Andrew D. Bernstein/Focus on Sports, Inc.)

Magic scores against the Celtics.

(John McDonough/Focus on Sports, Inc.)

All-star Larry Bird, holding his MVP trophy.

(Richard Pilling/Focus on Sports, Inc.)

Larry Bird stands alone.

Red Auerbach with Bird and teammates.

6
Hoosier Hysteria

Larry Joe Bird was born on December 7, 1956. He was Joe and Georgia Bird's third son and fourth child. Eventually, two more boys, Jeff and Eddie, were to join the three older brothers and sister, Linda.

Growing up in the midwestern valley that included West Baden and French Lick wasn't exactly easy, because there never seemed to be enough money.

The two towns are part of the rolling Indiana countryside, with beautifully wooded hills and gently sloping valleys. Tourism and furniture-making were the major sources of revenue, and the famous salt springs in the valley attracted enough seasonal tourists to help stabilize the area's otherwise sluggish economy.

There was, however, little money in the Bird home. Joe Bird worked for a piano company, as a furniture finisher. Ultimately, in a desperate attempt to keep her family on a sound financial basis, Georgia took a job as a cook in a restaurant. It required long hours, and the children learned to make do on their own.

By the time he reached school age, Larry was already nearly a head taller than most of his classmates. Teachers remember young Larry as fairly tough and somewhat aggressive, but also as incredibly shy and extremely concerned about the feelings of others.

Larry received little athletic encouragement from Joe Bird, who was divorced from Georgia while Larry was a teenager and later died a tragic death.

"I really just played for the fun of it," Larry remembers. "I think that's normal for a kid. Some people do it because they're looking ahead, making plans. I never knew what I was looking ahead to."

Springs Valley High School serves both West Baden and French Lick, the towns where Larry Bird was born and grew up. The coaches there remember him as a hard-working kid who needed a little discipline. Of course, that applies to many teenagers who really can't stand to be criticized, which, of course, coaches tend to do. Larry was booted off the eighth grade basketball team when he failed to show up for practice. Watching from the sidelines for the rest of the season, he learned a valuable lesson about a coach's authority. "He was extremely coachable after that," remembers coach Butch Emmons.

By his sophomore year at Springs Valley, Larry had shot up to 6 feet, 1 inch. But his weight never kept up. He was too skinny. Coach Jim Jones slotted Larry at guard, but he was, at that time, just an average player.

A serious injury early in his sophomore year taught Larry another valuable lesson. Sidelined by a broken left ankle, Larry was forced to observe, and that made him realize that the passing game was the key to overall team success. When he finally returned to the lineup, Larry, who had worked on his shooting while still in a cast and on crutches, got his first varsity assignment. It was in the closing seconds of a state tournament game, and he was fouled. The game was in the hands of Larry Bird.

He sank the shots, to help Springs Valley advance. "I had to make them," remembers Larry. "My brother Mark had never missed a free throw in the tournament. Family honor, you know."

Wearing Mark's old number, 33, Larry continued to improve as a junior. He underwent a weight program which helped put some much-needed weight on his bony frame. By that time, Larry had given up all his other sports, including baseball, even though his coaches thought he could become an outstanding pitcher.

Having grown to about 6 feet, 3 inches, and now weighing more than 150 pounds, Larry played nearly every position on the court for coach Jones. The combination of extra experience, extra size, and extra practice enabled him to become an outstanding ball-handler. He helped lead Springs Valley to a 19–2 season and another berth in the state tournament.

The summer between his junior and senior years of high school was, perhaps, the most important period in Larry Bird's life. Not because of anything he set out to do, however, but because of something he had no control over. Larry Bird grew about 4 inches.

When the next season started at Springs Valley, the word quickly spread. Larry Bird is unbelievable. And he was.

He was also unselfish on the court, which tended to upset his coaches. Coach Gary Holland recalls, "We couldn't get him to shoot enough. He preferred passing off. He seemed to get great satisfaction by setting up a teammate for a basket."

Fortunately, the disease wasn't fatal. Larry Joe managed to shoot enough to average 30.6 points per game and pull down around 20 rebounds per contest. The numbers made everyone, Springs Valley fans and opponents alike, blink.

College coaches began to take notice, as well. Suddenly, coaches from all over the midwest and other parts of the country were asking their secretaries to find out "how to get to French Lick, Indiana." Indiana's Bobby Knight was there more than a few times. Kentucky's Joe B. Hall showed up. So did Louisville's Denny Crum. Indiana State's Bob King was a frequent visitor. Sometimes there were enough coaches at a game to conduct a coaches' convention.

After a 17–3 season, Larry focused in on the long road to

Bloomington and the state finals. Bloomington, the home of Indiana University and Bobby Knight, was the goal of every high school player in the state. More than 600 teams would begin with the sectional round of play-offs, and each had Bloomington as its final goal.

Springs Valley won its sectional by knocking off host Paoli, whom they had already defeated twice earlier in the season, and Milltown. Larry scored 42 points in the two contests, far below his average.

In the regional semifinals, the Blackhawks just edged past Jasper, a team that they had clobbered during the regular season. That set up a regional final match against Bedford, a surprise finalist.

The Springs Valley Blackhawks were a narrow favorite. With little more than two minutes to go, the Blackhawks held what should have been a commanding 5-point lead.

In something over a minute, however, the Springs Valley lead dwindled to just one point. But Larry Bird was on the line for the Blackhawks, shooting one-and-one. He bounced the ball a couple of times, then tossed it at the orange ring. He missed.

The lead, which would have gone to three if Larry was successful, was gone moments later, when the Bedford center, fouled by Bird, canned 2 free throws. A few moments later, the final buzzer sounded, ending Springs Valley's hopes for a state championship and Larry Bird's high school career.

Though the season ended on a low note, Larry's career certainly did not. He won nearly every honor imaginable, set all sorts of statistical records, and was generally the most talked-about person in the neighborhood.

The summer would bring on new challenges, including all-star games against two challenging rivals—the Kentucky High School All-Stars and the Russian High School All-Stars. But first, the basketball world wanted to know the answer to a very important question: Where would Larry Bird spend his next four years? That answer would take more than a year to sort out.

7
Sycamore Power

Many young people, upon graduating from high school, search college catalogs and world atlases, looking for those fabled greener pastures. Larry Joe Bird, the pride of French Lick, Indiana, loved the pastures right there at home.

As a 6-foot, 8-inch, 200-pound all-star, with a long-range jump shot and an uncanny ability to pass a basketball to open teammates, Larry Bird could have gone to almost any college in the country. Larry Bird, on the other hand, had no great itch to travel.

Bird, who had worked on basketball — and little else—for the previous 6 or 7 years, actually did have his mind set on one school: the University of Kentucky, which is pretty close to Indiana. Kentucky is one of the most dominant schools in the world of college basketball, and the home of the late legendary coach, Adolph Rupp. Trouble was, coach Joe B. Hall, who succeeded Rupp, didn't really care for Larry. In more than a decade as UK coach, Hall didn't make many errors in judging player talent. Unfortunately, missing out on Larry Bird was a costly mistake.

Eventually, Larry boiled down his choices to three, all within the state of Indiana. It would have to be Indiana U., in Bloomington, or Purdue in Lafayette, or Indiana State in Terre Haute.

Everyone in French Lick and West Baden felt that Larry would do best at Indiana U. Indiana U. had a great basketball tradition, great media coverage, and one of the country's best and most famous coaches (Bob Knight). Knight, with the help of several of his famous stars, came to French Lick and charmed everyone, including Larry Bird.

It didn't take long for Larry to succumb to the pressure all around him. However, he had real concerns about going to Indiana U., where the student population was sixteen times the size of French Lick itself. Still, he knew that he would learn much from coach Knight, particularly about defense.

The major decision behind him—and aware that Kentucky, which didn't want him, was on Indiana's upcoming schedule—Larry went on to enjoy one of the best summers of his young life. As a member of the Indiana high school all-stars, he quickly showed everyone in the state that the small-town hick could more than hold his own with the big-city boys. Larry tossed in a dozen points and nabbed 9 rebounds in a 15-minute performance against the Russian high school stars as Indiana won 92–60. He followed that effort with a dozen more points in a 92–81 win over the Kentucky high school stars. Now no one, not even Joe B. Hall, the Kentucky coach, doubted Larry Bird.

Larry spent the rest of the summer with his friends back in West Baden, hanging around the local gas station.

When September rolled around, Larry packed up and moved to Bloomington. But he was never happy there. "It was too big," he recalled later. "I'd have to walk a mile to class. I couldn't hear anything because everyone seemed to be talking at once."

His basic shyness made him feel uncomfortable, so he quietly packed and returned to French Lick.

Indiana officials were frantic. Bird hadn't even informed coach Knight of his decision to leave. The folks in French Lick and West Baden were also deeply disappointed. They had hoped that their star would go on to great fame at IU and lead the Hoosiers to a national title. Now, he was back, hanging out at the gas station again, his basketball career apparently at an end. There were all sorts of rumors. "Larry can't cut it with Knight," said one. "Knight ran him off because of his attitude," said another. In truth, Larry never even went to a practice, which, according to NCAA regulations, could not begin until October 15.

Larry enrolled at Northwood Institute, a junior college in West Baden. But he couldn't become accustomed to the discipline of attending classes and soon dropped out. Next he went to work for the town of French Lick, driving a truck and hauling garbage.

He stayed active in basketball by hooking up with an amateur team and won the MVP trophy at the 1975 AAU basketball tournament. One college coach, Bob King, at Indiana State, hadn't forgotten Larry.

Larry really didn't want to go back to college, but the coaches got plenty of support from Larry's fans in West Baden and French Lick. They kept reminding Larry that he'd been "a quitter" when he left Indiana U. Larry's mother agreed with them, and even his grandmother jumped on the bandwagon. Larry was finally convinced. He told King that he'd be coming to ISU.

That fall, Larry began to find himself. He knew that he would have to skip the upcoming season. According to NCAA rules, a transfer student must sit out a year before becoming eligible for athletics. With Larry on the sidelines, ISU struggled through a 13–12 season, which, in itself, was an improvement over the two previous seasons. Still, knowing that Bird would be leading the Sycamores the following season, there was plenty of excitement on the campus.

The fatherly approach of coach King had provided great leadership through Larry's troubled times. Larry repaid him by working hard, really hard, polishing his skills and helping mold the team, and when Larry's ISU career finally began, the once-empty seats at the Hulman Arena suddenly began to fill up.

With Larry scoring bucketfuls of points, the Sycamores quickly lost their image as patsies. They were actually blowing folks away. A month and a half into their season, Larry poured in 47 points to set a school record and lead ISU to a big win over Missouri-St. Louis. With 16 wins in their first 17 outings, the Sycamores moved into the Top 20 ratings. And when they finished their season at 25–2, they earned the school's first-ever major-college tournament bid, from the National Invitation Tournament, the oldest post-season basketball tournament. A 1-point loss at the University of Houston was disappointing, but it only set the stage for the season to come.

Between seasons, Larry Bird became absolutely the biggest thing on the ISU campus. If you believed his clippings, he was, arguably, the best college basketball player in the land. Still, Larry took on none of the flamboyance of other superstars. He dressed simply, lived simply, acted simply. But how long could anyone sporting a scoring average of more than 32 points per game and 13.3 rebounds per outing stay humble? In Larry Bird's case, forever. He was the complete team player, unselfish, a pinpoint passer, filled with game savvy, court sense, and smarts.

But Larry's second college season would prove to be a disappointment. Thanks to their Big Bird, the Sycamores had managed to nudge into the select group of Indiana college powerhouses, along with Indiana, Purdue, Notre Dame, and the like. They were the heavy favorites in the Missouri Valley Conference. And they knocked off Purdue and its 7-foot, 2-inch center Joe Barry Carroll, breaking a string of 24 Purdue victories in the last 25 games against ISU. The final score was 91–63. The Sycamores were for real.

In fact, ISU won its first 13 games and reached the number 4 slot on the Associated Press weekly poll before losing its first game to Southern Illinois. But that was the beginning of the end. Despite Bird's heroics and a 20 ppg performance from Harry Morgan, ISU couldn't put it together again. They finished second in the league, second in the conference play-offs, and lost to Rutgers in the National Invitation Tournament. The demise of the Sycamores was distressing. It brought everyone on the campus back down to earth.

And then came the news that the Boston Celtics had drafted Larry on the first round of the NBA draft.

The Celtics and their dynamic leader, Red Auerbach, would have to wait. Larry Bird decided that he owed Indiana State another season. The coaches at State and the team's fans were thrilled.

Despite Larry's presence, the new season opened with little fanfare. Coach King, after suffering an off-season heart attack, was gone, replaced by assistant coach Hodges. And Bird was the Sycamores' only returning starter.

Despite their lack of experience and of a true big man at center, the Sycamores started winning and kept winning. Big Alex Gilbert began grabbing rebounds; Speedy Carl Nicks, who had doubts about his ability to play big-time basketball, controlled himself and the team from the point-guard position. And Bird at power forward was never better.

Again, ISU won its first 13 games and again was ranked number 4 in the nation. But this time there was no disaster. Larry averaged more than 32 points per game, and they continued to roll, while, one by one, the higher-ranked teams tasted defeat. When ISU won its eighteenth straight game, it reached number 2.

But disaster almost did strike in the nineteenth game. The Sycamores trailed New Mexico State by 83–81 with only 3 seconds to go. New Mexico State had a one-and-one opportunity on the line, with a chance to salt away the victory. And Bird was on the bench, after fouling out of his first college game. The Sycamores needed a miracle.

They got it. The foul shot was missed, ISU got the rebound, Brad Miley got the ball to Bobby Heaton at mid-court, and Heaton heaved up a prayer. Miracle time. The ball smacked off the backboard and dropped through the hoop.

Having tied the score, ISU was really pumped up and, even though they were "Birdless," went on to win in overtime, and their undefeated streak continued.

Now ranked number 1 in the country, the Sycamores rolled into the conference tournament final game against New Mexico State. Playing at home, ISU managed to build a comfortable lead when the unthinkable occurred. Larry Bird fractured his thumb. His team went on to win the game, retain the top ranking, and gain the top seed in the NCAA Midwest Regional. But no one knew if Larry could play in the tournament. And, even if he could, how well could he play?

While honors, including several Player of the Year awards, began pouring in for Bird, Larry's practices were severely curtailed. As the opening round of the tournament arrived, there were still questions about how well he could play with an injury.

Early in the game against Virginia Tech at Lawrence, Kansas, the Sycamores fell behind as Larry went without a rebound for nearly 10 minutes. Then suddenly he and ISU got it going. He was rebounding, passing, and scoring as if nothing had ever been wrong. ISU soared to a 17-point win, its thirtieth of the season. "This tournament," thought Larry Bird, "could be fun."

And it was. At the regional championships in Cincinnati, ISU ran up an impressive and easy victory over Oklahoma and an even more impressive but incredibly tough 2-pointer over highly regarded Arkansas. Larry had 31 in that nail-biter, and Bob Heaton once again hit the winner with 2 seconds to go.

That brought the Sycamores to the famous Final Four, which was going to be played at the University of Utah in Salt Lake City. It was Bird and ISU vs. powerful DePaul and Magic Johnson and Michigan State vs. surprising Penn. That Magic and his mates blew away the Quakers in one semifinal was not surprising. And it was no surprise that DePaul and Indiana State went right down to the wire.

Bird, despite aggravating his thumb injury, was astounding. He scored 23 points in the first half, as ISU maintained a narrow lead. Then, in the closing minutes, the lead seesawed back and forth. First, Indiana State; then, DePaul. A last-second attempt by DePaul's All-American, Mark Aguirre, fell just off the mark, and a free-throw and a second later, ISU had a 76–74 win and a berth against Magic and his Spartans in the title game. Larry Bird's semifinal contribution: would you believe 16 of 19 from the field, 35 points, and 16 boards?

The match up of Johnson and Bird triggered immense interest all around the country in the MSU-ISU NCAA championship game. The Spartans of Michigan State were narrowly favored, despite the fact that their opponents were unbeaten in 33 tries and ranked number 1. That was because many experts felt that State, with two great players, Johnson and Greg Kelser (and Jay Vincent as well), would overcome the team with only a single superstar, Bird.

The real hero for Michigan State, however, was coach Jud Heathcote, whose strategy of using a blanketing zone defense shut Bird down. The Spartans were all over Larry, right from the opening tip-off, and it was never really close.

Limited to 19 points and hitting only 7 of 21 field-goal attempts, Larry wasn't able to rally his team. Though the Sycamores made one brief run in the second half, it was all MSU. The Spartans eased to an 11-point victory.

Larry was distraught, of course. His shooting touch—forget the injured thumb—had deserted him just when he needed it most. Still, he and his teammates and his coaches had nearly done the impossible. The people of Terre Haute, home of ISU, were still on a high when the Sycamores returned from Utah. The gala celebration would have hardly been more joyous if the team had beaten Michigan State.

The folks in French Lick were even happier. Now there were two things that made their town famous—the salt springs *and* Larry Bird.

8
Beantown

If there's one word that best describes Arnold (Red) Auerbach, it's shrewd. Throughout his more than 30 years at the helm of the NBA's Boston Celtics, Auerbach has consistently made the right draft pick, the right coaching move, the right trade, all of which has kept the green-and-white club on the road to championship after championship. By winning eight titles in a row between 1959 and 1966, coach Auerbach put together the greatest dynasty in the history of professional sports. And as team president, after his coaching career ended, Auerbach has continued to push the right button nearly every time. Sure, there have been down years here and there, but Auerbach always figured a way to right the Celtic ship before it plunged anywhere near the NBA's depths. He is considered by most experts to be the best basketball mind of all time. He has consistently managed to obtain the right players to mold into a championship team, and he has usually outfoxed rivals in trades, as when he obtained Bill Russell, considered to be the best defensive center of all time, and the key player in four championship seasons, from the St. Louis (now Atlanta) Hawks.

Throughout the 1978-79 basketball season, Auerbach kept a

close eye on the goings-on around the Hulman Arena in Terre Haute, Ind. Truth is, things weren't pretty in Boston, and Red was deeply concerned. The 1977–78 Celtics, in one of their rare losing seasons, had gone 32–50 and finished third in their division, 23 games out of first. They missed the NBA play-offs for the first time since 1971. And the 1978–79 season was worse. Boston was 29–53, fifth in its division, and 25 games out of first place.

There were rumblings in Beantown. The old master has lost it, his critics claimed. He was no longer making the trade or the draft pick that could rescue the stumbling ball club. The Celtics were through.

Forget it. Cagey Red Auerbach knew that salvation was on the way. The more he watched Indiana State and Larry Bird, the more convinced he was that he was within a cashier's check—with plenty of zeroes—of returning the Celtics to the top of the NBA.

It took the biggest rookie package in the history of the NBA—approximately $3.25 million over 5 years—but Red finally got his man. The Celtics introduced their prize at one of the best-attended news conferences anyone in Boston could remember. Larry, overcoming his basic shyness, and, no doubt, filled with some of the confidence that comes with earning more than $600,000 per year, had all the right answers. When one reporter asked him if he was happy with the money package, Larry grinned and said, "Don't tell Red, but I love basketball so much I'd have played for nothing."

Not likely, but the money never went—and still hasn't gone—to Larry's head. To this day, he seems to prefer French Lick to the big cities which he visits while earning his hefty living. "I want to help take care of my mom," said Larry at the signing ceremony. "She deserves it."

Throughout the summer, as Larry got ready for his first Celtic season, the critics—you can never get rid of them—had a field day. Auerbach was taken, some of them charged. Bird isn't quick enough, or tough enough, can't jump high enough, or shoot well enough, can't play defense adequately to make it big in the NBA.

Red Auerbach laughed and took a puff on his famous trademark, a cigar. Let the critics have their say now, Red knew that Larry Bird was a franchise player who would turn the team around. The only question was how soon could he turn around a team that had compiled a 29–53 record—one of the worst in the NBA—during the previous season.

The pressure to produce so much so quickly could have made a lesser man crumble. Before he donned the Celtic green-and-white for the first time, newsmen and fans in Boston were already referring to the upcoming years as The Bird Years. There had been the Cousy Years, when Bob Cousy was cavorting in the Celtic backcourt, and the Russell Years, when lanky Bill Russell was swatting away opponents' shots while earning five MVP awards.

With Archibald and bull's-eye shooter Chris Ford at guard, Bird and Cedric Maxwell at forward, and a more relaxed Dave Cowens at center, the Celts opened with a tough 8-point win over the Houston Rockets. Instantly, Larry began doing the things people expected of him. He made the big pass, and he triggered the famed Celtic fast break. He hit the key shot, which had been missing for the last couple of years; he grabbed the important rebound.

Scoring nearly 20 points per game, grabbing more than 10 rebounds, dashing off nearly 6 assists, he had the Celtics playing winning and exciting basketball. Magic may have been playing in Los Angeles, but there was another magician back in Boston.

Johnson and Bird, who had been closely linked in their battle for the college championship and college all-star honors, became even more closely tied in the pros. On those rare occasions when the Celtics and Lakers were matched on the court, the press had a field day. Would Larry be especially fired up to avenge his college loss to Johnson's team? Would Magic be more excited than usual to gain revenge for Bird's college Player-of-the-Year honors? The result was lots of media attention and, of course, packed arenas.

Both players tended to play down their rivalry. Their head-to-head match ups weren't really match ups. Neither guarded the other. In fact, with Johnson at guard and Bird at forward, they didn't even play the same position. Still, reporters took careful note of the Lakers' two victories in two tries over Boston, despite the fact that neither Johnson nor Bird dominated either game.

Those two losses, amazingly enough, represented nearly 10 percent of the Celtics' losses during the 1979–80 season. In one of the most incredible turnarounds in sports history, the Celts went from 29–53 and last place in their division to 61–21 and first place. After a two-year lapse, Boston was back in the play-offs, ready to add another championship banner to the collection which flies high above Boston Garden.

The Celts' 4–0 shellacking of Houston in the opening round was evidence that it could happen. Boston was overwhelming, winning by 18 and 20 at home, then by 19 and 15 in Texas. The Celts totally shut down Houston Rockets' superstar Moses Malone, causing the Rockets' coach Del Harris to rave about his conquerors, "They're the best I've seen."

Much of the credit for Harris's review went to Bird. "What makes him so great," said one close observer, "is that he makes the rest of the team play so well." They'd been saying that about Larry all the way back at Springs Valley High. Unselfish, dynamic, hardworking. They called Larry a blue-collar player, because he wasn't afraid to work hard, to dive for the loose ball, and to outhustle the rest of the bunch. Like a steelworker with his lunch pail under his arm, when the whistle blows, Larry Bird goes to work.

Next in line were the Philadelphia 76ers. In the play-off opener, at the Boston Garden, Larry had 27 points, but the Celts shot horribly and Philly pulled off a 96–93 victory. Although Boston won the second game, as Larry and Dave Cowens sparkled, the 96–90 victory was the last of the Celts' season.

Despite game-high efforts of 22 and 19 points by Bird, the Celtics fell, 99–97 and 102–90 in games 3 and 4. The season ended quietly in Boston Garden when the Celtics, down three games to one, fell 105–104. No more miracles, no more comebacks. It was over for the Celtics. But as spring turned to summer in Boston, Larry Bird resolved to do whatever it took to prevent a repeat occurrence the following season.

9
Not Always a Bridesmaid

During the summer Larry returned to the slower pace of life in French Lick, Indiana, armed with more money, more fame, and more awards than he had ever imagined possible. He had won almost every conceivable honor during his rookie season. The twenty-two-year-old had been selected Rookie of the Year, been unanimously voted to the All-Rookie team, finished third in the Most Valuable Player balloting, and won a spot on the All-NBA first team.

But none of this turned Larry Bird's head for a moment. He is blessed with what New York Knick coach Hubie Brown calls "enormous work capacity." That's how Hubie judges a player's honesty. How hard does he work and how often? Larry Bird scores high in both categories.

So with the stinging defeat still growing at him, Larry went home to Indiana, to his mother and his friends, to the gas station in West Baden, and to the courts where he could begin working to prevent another play-off failure. Larry was tired—tired of seasons without a championship. Springs Valley High had just missed in the Indiana state high school championships. Indiana State had been a high-flying but second-place finisher in the NCAA tournament. And now the Celtics, off an outstanding season, hadn't been able to battle past Philadelphia.

He spent long hours polishing his moves and increasing his endurance. When the 1980–81 season rolled around, he would be ready.

So were the Celtics. Red Auerbach had been busy, too. He had pried Robert Parish away from the Golden State Warriors. The 7 foot Parish would give the Celts something they had been lacking—real size in the middle. And Red picked 6-foot, 1-inch Kevin McHale in the first round of the draft. The left-handed shooting graduate from the University of Minnesota was, like Bird, a blue-collar player, the kind who dived for every loose ball, who scrapped for every loose ball and banged the boards. The Celts were ready to go again.

Throughout the 1980–81 season, the Celts were locked into a fierce duel with the 76ers for the Eastern Conference title. The Sixers kept winning and so did the Celtics. Larry's versatile play and his talent for coming through in the clutch kept Boston in the hunt. The clutch performance is often taken for granted. Yet NBA coaches can give you a list of normally outstanding players who will run away and hide when a key basket is needed in the final seconds of a game.

When a Celtic game was on the line, that's when Larry wanted the ball most. And first place was on the line down the entire stretch in 1981. Thanks to Larry's incredible play, Boston ran off a string of 25 wins in 26 games, which gave Boston a share of the Eastern title with Philadelphia. Each team finished 62–20, an improvement of one game over Larry's rookie year.

Bird also improved in every statistical category—except scoring. Playing in the full 82 games of each year, Larry scored 1,745 points his first year and "only" 1,741 the second. His average "plummeted" from 21.3 to 21.2 points per game. But he improved in field goal percentage (47.4 percent to 47.8 percent), free-throw percentage (83.6 percent to 86.3 percent), rebounds (852 to 895), assists (370 to 451), steals (143 to 161), and blocked shots (53 to 63).

When play-off time rolled around, Bird was steeled for a supreme effort. He was not content to finish anywhere but on top. There had been too many runner-up trophies in the past.

The opening round was a breeze. The Chicago Bulls, who had struggled into the play-offs, lost four straight.

That set up a meeting with Philadelphia. The Sixers team was essentially made up of the same players who had eliminated Boston in their previous two play-off meetings. And they beat the Celts in the opening game, 105-104, on a pair of Andrew Toney freethrows with two seconds remaining on the clock.

Boston could not afford to lose in game 2. Larry Bird responded to the situation with a 34-point effort, which led Boston to a 118-99 victory. But it doesn't matter whether you win by 1 point or by 19; the series was tied, 1-1.

The Celtics were never really in game 3, as Philly coasted to a 110-100 victory. And game 4 seemed just as grim. The Sixers led by 18 in the second half and were playing with the confidence of proven winners.

Boston began to chip away at the lead. It was down to 10, then to 8, up to 10, then down to 6. Still, the Sixers had the clock on their side, and those valuable seconds were ticking away.

With less than 30 seconds to go, Boston trimmed the margin to 107-105. But that was as close as they were going to get. A second later the buzzer sounded. Philly's 107-105 win put the Celtics in a sudden-death situation. One more loss, and the season would be over.

In the 3 days that followed, newsmen had a field day, recounting how few teams had ever come back from a 3-1 deficit. For Larry Bird, another season with a frustrating end appeared at hand.

But the Bird wasn't ready to end his season. "We can beat them three straight," Larry told friends, fully aware that the Celts hadn't beaten them three straight in years and hadn't won a single game in the Spectrum, the 76ers home court, in more than two seasons.

To get a shot at winning game 6 in the Spectrum, however, the Celtics would first have to win game 5 in Boston. With little more than a minute and a half to go, that didn't seem likely. The Sixers were clinging to a 6-point lead, 109–103. The 15,000 fans in Boston Garden were silent.

But a few moments later excitement returned when an Andrew Toney miss at one end was converted into a driving lay-up at the other end by Boston's Tiny Archibald. Whistle! Foul! Tiny stepped to the line and canned the free-throw. Suddenly it was 109–106. The Celtics had a chance, a long shot of course, but a chance nevertheless.

Philly ball—the Sixers rushed down the court as the clock ran down on the Celtics. The ball went to Toney, but Andrew's jump shot was stuffed by the lanky Robert Parish.

Back came the Celtics. Larry Bird drove toward the hoop. Twisting as he moved, he tossed up a shot that swished through the net. 109–108. Everyone in the Boston Garden was on his feet, and the roar of 15,000 screaming fans was almost deafening.

Now the 76ers felt the pressure, felt the Celtics breathing down their necks. The clock continued to flash, 0:45, 0:44, 0:43. A sloppy pass from Dr. J was picked off by Bird. The Celtics had the ball and a chance to take the lead. The noise in the Garden grew louder.

As the clock continued to tick down, the ball went to Bird on the right and on the run. He put up a carom shot off of the backboard. The ball bounced off the glass, bounced off the rim, bounded high in the air, and was grabbed off by M. L. Carr. A whistle sounded a foul on the Sixers. Carr stepped up to the line and, with a mountain of pressure on his shoulders, tossed in 2 foul shots, giving Boston the lead. The Garden was shaking from the noise generated by the howling Boston fans, who had seen their team turn a 6-point defeat into a 1-point lead in little more than a minute. As the Sixers moved the ball up the court, the clock read

0:20. They had the ball and could win on a last shot. Double-teamed by Bird and Parish, Bobby Jones put up a last-gasp jumper that failed. Carr once again grabbed the rebound and was fouled. M. L.'s free-throw iced it. The Celtics won 111 – 109.

Bird's fifth-game performance, consisting of 32 points, 11 boards, and 5 assists, had kept the Celts in the hunt. Now he would have to do it all over again in Philadelphia, the City of Brotherly Love.

He did it, although once again, it had looked impossible for a while, as Boston fell behind by 17 points early in the game. But the Celts came back. Fired up and led by Larry's 25-point effort, they rallied to win by a single bucket, 100 – 98.

Now the series was even at three apiece, with the deciding game back in Boston. The game was shown on network television to an audience of many millions, but no group had more interest in the outcome than the Houston Rockets—the Cinderella team—the surprise winners in the Western Conference play-offs, who were waiting to play the winners of this series.

If the Celtics knew an easy way to win, they certainly didn't show it. Once again, Boston allowed Philadelphia to move out to an early double-figure lead. Boston kept coming back, but then Philly would extend the lead again. Boston never managed to come back enough to even the game, though. Midway through the final period, the Sixers still clung to a 6-point lead.

Larry Bird, faced with extreme pressure, was never better. He had to be, because Dr. J was putting on an amazing performance of his own, swooping, leaping, gliding, scoring. But Bird and his teammates never gave up. Larry's steal of a Dr. J pass produced one bucket. The lead shrunk to 4, then to 2.

Another steal gave Boston another opportunity. Larry drove to the right side, threw up an off-balance shot; it missed, but he was fouled by Erving. Bird calmly hit both shots, and suddenly the game was tied at 89.

Then, just as quickly, both teams went cold. Each had several opportunities to break the tie, but both failed. With just over a minute left, Philly's massive Darryl Dawkins threw up an airball that missed everything. Bird grabbed the ball and zipped down the court. He thought about going to the basket. But Julius Erving had cut the lane off, so Larry pulled up and, soaring over Erving, flicked up a one-hander that banked off the glass and swished into the net. The 12-foot shot gave Boston a 91–89 lead. The Eastern title, the road to the finals, were all within the Celtics' grasp. Unfortunately 48 seconds still remained, less than a minute on a clock, but an eternity in a pro basketball game.

A misfired pass gave Boston the ball again, but Philly's Mo Cheeks stole it back and moved in for the tying bucket. But a foul by Gerald Henderson caused him to miss the shot, and Cheeks was able to hit only 1 of the 2 free throws. Boston still led 91–90. After a Celtic miss, Philly got the ball back with 1 second to go. A desperation shot hit the backboard and caromed to Maxwell. It was over. For the first time in 2 hours, the crowd in the Garden was able to breathe. Their shouts were heard all the way down in Philadelphia. The Celtics, miraculously, were moving on—to the the finals, against the Rockets.

Larry Bird's shot had been the winner, capping a 7-game series that saw him raise his scoring average to 26.7 points per game.

Though the Celtics had "owned" the Houston Rockets, having beaten them fourteen straight, you would almost expect a letdown following the fierce series with the Sixers. It almost happened.

It took some closing-minutes heroics by Bird to rally the Celtics in game 1, 98–95. With just under 4 minutes remaining, Boston trailed 87–84. Larry shook open for a 20-foot jumper from the right side. Ever alert, Larry instantly realized that the shot would be off, so he headed for the right baseline, hoping for the rebound. It came off of the rim just as he'd anticipated. He grabbed it in the air, but he was falling toward the end line. So, while he was falling out of bounds, he shifted the ball to his left hand and tossed up a left-handed shot that swished through the hoop. Even the other pros were stunned by that play.

It was the turning point in an important game. Houston never really recovered, though a brief Rocket run at the end was snuffed out by another Bird shot.

That win loomed even larger when Houston won game 2, at Boston Garden, 92–90. The teams split again in Houston, returning the home-court edge to Boston. The Celts clobbered the Rockets in game 3, 94–71, but, led by Moses Malone, Houston evened the series by taking game 4, 91–86.

As the teams returned to Boston, the Rockets were supremely confident. They taunted the Celtics, belittling their rivals. Bird had suffered in Houston, scoring only 8 points per game. Robert Reid of the Rockets had been staying right in Bird's socks. It seemed as though he'd started guarding him when Bird left the team bus and he never let up.

That all changed in game 5. Boston blew the Rockets away, 109–80, then secured the title, Larry Bird's first, with a 102–91 win back in Houston. Larry scored 27 points in that game, including a crucial 3-point play that helped put the game away.

Another championship banner was ordered for the Boston Garden rafters. And the frustration of always finishing second was over for Larry Bird. He had his championship. He would never have to make an excuse again.

10
The Hick from French Lick

If there was ever a doubt about Larry Bird, the 1980–81 NBA championship erased it. His productivity, his versatility, his leadership, and his great courage handling pressure proved conclusively that he was a champion. There were still plenty of votes for Dr. J, and you'd never convince the Magic Johnson fans, but Larry was deemed the best by most of the NBA. Veteran coach Kevin Loughery summed it up when he said, "He's simply the best we [the NBA] have."

Larry continued to thrive in Boston, at least on the court, although he still wasn't comfortable with big-city life or big-city media. In NBA locker rooms, the press is admitted 10 minutes after each game. The trainer's room, however, is off- limits. Most of the Celtic starters take advantage of this safe area, for varying lengths of time. This doesn't thrill reporters for morning newspapers, who must meet incredibly tight deadlines. Still, it is a fact of life and is accepted by both sides. Invariably, the last Celtic to leave the haven of the trainer's table is Bird, who still winds up facing a large chorus of questioners. But it does reduce the time that reporters have to ask their questions.

"I'd rather do it that way," says Bird, "instead of answering the same question over and over."

Although he remains comparatively withdrawn, Bird continues to grow in stature in the NBA. The 1981–82 season, for instance, brought a team record of 18 consecutive wins, and Larry was voted MVP of the league All-Star Game. He won that by scoring 12 of the East team's final 16 points in a virtual one-man show.

But following the 1981 championship, there were some disappointments. Bird was injured—reported by some to be a fractured jaw, by others an injured cheek. Sidelined for 5 games late in the season, he remained inactive for the longest period in his professional career.

And Philadelphia garnered a measure of revenge when the Sixers knocked out the Celtics in the Eastern finals of the 1982 play-offs. As in 1981, Philly moved off to a 3–1 lead by winning one game in Boston and sweeping a pair in Philadelphia. Just when it looked as though the Celts were coming back (winning game 5, 114–85, and game 6 in Philadelphia, 88–75), Billy Cunningham's Sixers slammed the door, with a resounding 120–106 victory in Boston.

Meanwhile, selecting Larry to the All-NBA Team was becoming a habit. And why not? He seemed to improve in every area, every year. In 1981–82, he raised his scoring to 22.9 and improved his shooting percentage, from 47.8 percent to 50.3 percent. All that hard work had paid off.

Larry wasn't—and isn't—a pretty shooter. His shot is fairly flat, his elbow flails off at an unlikely angle, but the ball does go in. All those hours in the Springs Valley gym, on the court (now complete with glass backboards) next to his house in French Lick, at the Celtics' practice court at Hellenic College, and at the Boston Garden had proved worthwhile.

Today, when Celtics' players show up at 6 P.M. for a 7:30 game, they're usually arriving an hour after Larry. "I take so many crazy shots, I've just got to work on them," he says.

The old Celtic great, Bill Russell, is one of Bird's greatest admirers. Russell never doubted that that fall-away, left-handed shot Bird had hit to win that crucial game with Houston in 1980 would go in. "Larry knew it would go in," said the bearded giant, "because he had rehearsed it in his mind hundreds of times before."

The Celtics showed some signs of slipping during the 1982–1983 season. They struggled through a 56–26 season, not exactly a disaster but not up to their standards or the expectations of their fans. And they finished 9 games behind the hated 76ers and quickly bowed out in the play-offs.

Though Boston had disposed of Atlanta in a tough best-of-three mini-series, the Milwaukee Bucks absolutely embarrassed them in the Eastern semifinals. For the first time in history, the Celts fell in four straight.

Bird, though, continued to soar. He had a club record 53 points in one game against the Indiana Pacers. He raised his per-game scoring to 23.6 (eleventh in the league). And he ranked among the league leaders in steals (148), free-throw percentage (.840), and rebounds (870).

Despite Bird's success, the second-place season finish was more than Celtic management could handle. At season's end, they said good-bye to coach Bill Fitch and hello to former Celtic great, K. C. Jones. If anyone in Boston was ever placed on the hot seat, it was the likeable K. C.

Before the 1984 season began, Larry's attorney negotiated a new long-term contract that gave Larry financial peace of mind. It made the Celtics feel pretty good, too, since they could afford to lose Larry as much as Metropolis could afford to lose Superman. Financial security never affected his game, as it has with so many other pros. It didn't make him run any faster. It didn't increase his vertical jump. It didn't increase his shooting accuracy. And it certainly didn't diminish his love for winning, or his ability to help his teammates get the most out of their respective talents.

Former Celtic Dave Cowens put it very well: "I don't know what it is about Bird that makes him so special," the redhead told *The Christian Science Monitor*'s Phil Elderkin. "But it's something mental that other players with more physical talent don't have. When it comes to creating good situations for other people, he's almost in a class by himself."

The regular season was a welcome breath of fresh air for Bird. With quieter leadership from K. C. Jones and the multidimensional play of guard Dennis Johnson, who had been obtained from Phoenix—Red Auberbach had struck again—the Celts soared back to the top of the NBA East. With a 62–20 record, Boston won their division by 10 games, a 19-game turnaround from the previous year.

For his part, Bird once again led his team in almost every statistical category, finishing tenth in the league in rebounding (10.1 per game), first in foul shooting (88.8 percent), and seventh in scoring (24.2). He also led the league's forwards in assists (6.6 per game).

Larry's specialty was the double-double and triple-double game. A double-double game means that a player achieves double figures (10 or more) in scoring and rebounding. A triple-double game means achieving double figures in scoring, rebounding, and assists. Larry played 79 games during the season (he missed 3 games with stretched knee ligaments and a back/shoulder injury). He had 45 double-double games and 7 triple doubles.

But he saved the best for last—the play-offs. Thanks to the expanded NBA play-offs, the road to a world championship was now longer and more difficult to negotiate.

The traditional two-of-three mini-series was now three-of-five (and the division champs no longer received a free pass in the first round). Boston struggled hard to eliminate the upstart Washington Bullets in four games, winning the clincher in Washington after an overtime win by the Bullets in game 3.

They met the rejuvenated New York Knicks next. Hubie Brown, master of the work ethic, had coaxed the most out of his group and benefited from the superb scoring of Bernard King. Everyone looked forward to King versus Bird, with the possible exception of King and Bird.

It turned out that the home-court advantage was all the Celtics needed, but not before they got the scare of their lives. When New York won game 6, 106–104, the series was deadlocked at three apiece. Each victory had occurred on the winner's home court. That set up a deciding contest on the Boston Garden floor.

Bird saw to it that New York never really had a chance. He tossed in his all-time play-off high of 39 points, grabbed 12 rebounds, and passed for 10 assists. He had made another triple-double when the chips were down. Bird had outrebounded his rival, King, by 74 to 34 and, somewhat surprisingly, outscored him as well.

When Boston gained revenge against Milwaukee for last year's sweep in the play-offs, winning 4 games to 1, the stage was set for another highly anticipated battle for the title. For Larry Bird, the match up was perfect. It was Magic Johnson and the Lakers. The two superstars, linked since the 1979 college season, have been compared constantly despite playing different positions for different types of teams in two of the most different cities in the league.

As the play-offs approached, both players downplayed their roles in the Johnson-Bird battle. They had performed their act so often that you could almost predict their answers to media questions.

"C'mon, it's not a one-on-one game. It's five-on-five."

"I play forward and he plays guard. I don't guard him and he doesn't guard me."

Those were the public statements. Inside, each knew that no matter what they said, comparisons would be made. And each, as a total pro, wanted to come out on top.

The first game of the series went to Johnson and the Lakers. Los Angeles came out firing, quickly jumping to a 24–9 lead. Johnson, guarded by Gerald Henderson, who gave away 7 inches to the Magic Man, hit his first four shots. Bird, guarded closely by Michael Cooper, had to work harder than usual, and with less than usual success. Though Bird helped Boston climb back to within

105–101 in the last five minutes, L. A. pulled away to win comfortably, 115–109. However, the day belonged to Kareem Abdul-Jabbar, the Lakers' thirty-seven-year-old center, who scored 32 points.

Then Boston bounced back with a hairbreadth overtime victory in game 2, headlined by Bird's 27 points and 13 rebounds. Fearful of falling two behind at home, Larry and his mates had succeeded when it counted.

The series went back and forth. Bird's 30 points in game 3 at Los Angeles were wasted, as the Lakers romped, 137–104. The Celtics were plainly embarrassed and in great danger of returning home down 3 games to 1.

But, with Larry scoring 29 points and grabbing a personal play-off high of 21 rebounds, the Celtics got even on another overtime mind-bender, 129–125. It was becoming habit-forming. Los Angeles would win a blowout, Boston would tie it up and win in a spine tingler. And it was Bird, double-doubling in every game, who was keeping Boston alive.

Now it was back to Boston, the series having been reduced to the best-of-the-remaining-three. The Celtics once again owned the home-court advantage, but previous results were proving that edge rather useless.

Larry continued to score as he had never scored before. In the fifth game, he led Boston in scoring for the fourth straight game, hitting for 34 while grabbing 17 rebounds. For the first time, Boston had what the players call "a laugher"—an easy win. The 121–103 victory had been secured reasonably early in the game.

Now the Lakers had their backs to the wall. And the great Kareem had a hot night, 30 points and 10 rebounds, to help the Lakers to a 119–108 victory. Larry's numbers—28 points and 14 boards—weren't bad either, just not enough.

As it has so often since the Celts won their first title in 1957, the series came down to game 7 in Boston. There had been 14 other titles since 1957, each represented by the ever-present banners in the Boston Garden rafters. Now, at home, Larry Bird and

Co. would try for number 15.

On a warm Tuesday night, June 12, 1984, in the ancient, un-air-conditioned, musty Garden, Larry and his mates "owned" the famous parquet floor. Larry scored "only" 20 points (nearly 7½ points under his average for the 7-game series), but he made the key buckets and got plenty of help from Cedric Maxwell (24 points) and Robert Parish (16 rebounds). The fifteenth banner was ready to join the original fourteen. Boston won, 111–102, and the rivalry with Magic Johnson had been revved up just a bit more.

The following year, the tables would be turned. Bird, hampered by an injured hand, couldn't do enough to keep the Lakers away. Kareem, Magic, and Co. won twice in Boston and clinched the title with a 111–100 win in L. A. Larry had 28 points in the finale but missed on 17 of his 29 shots. It wasn't his best performance.

As he has matured, Bird has grown both on and off the court. He handles the press with greater ease and deals with his fame better. Now realizing that he can be himself and be respected and accepted, he no longer runs off and hides from the public.

He's still basically a simple fellow, whose heart remains in French Lick where, he has said, he'd like to coach junior high school basketball when his playing days are over.

The basketball-shaped street sign, larger than the signs at service stations, looms high over the hill in French Lick. In letters 2 feet high, the sign reads LARRY BIRD BLVD. That's where Larry is happiest, where it all began and where he wants it to end.

MAGIC JOHNSON

Michigan State University Record

Year	G.	Min.	FGA	FGM	Pct.	FTA	FTM	Pct.	Reb.	Pts.	Avg.
77-78	30	.....	382	175	.458	205	161	.785	237	511	17.0
78-79	32	1159	370	173	.468	240	202	.842	234	548	17.1
Totals	62	.....	752	348	.463	445	363	.816	471	1059	17.1

NBA Regular Season Record

Season—Team	G.	Min.	FGA	FGM	Pct.	FTA	FTM	Pct.	Ast.	PF	Dq.	Stl.	Blk.	Pts.	Avg.
79-80—Los Angeles	77	2795	949	503	.530	462	374	.810	563	218	1	187	41	1387	18.0
80-81—Los Angeles	37	1371	587	312	.532	225	171	.760	317	100	0	127	27	798	21.6
81-82—Los Angeles	78	2991	1036	556	.537	433	329	.760	743	223	1	208	34	1447	18.6
82-83—Los Angeles	79	2907	933	511	.548	380	304	.800	829	200	1	176	47	1326	16.8
83-84—Los Angeles	67	2567	780	441	.565	358	290	.810	875	169	1	150	49	1178	17.6
84-85—Los Angeles	77	2781	899	504	.561	464	391	.843	968	155	0	113	25	1406	18.3
Totals	415	15412	5184	2827	.545	2322	1859	.801	4295	1065	4	961	223	7542	18.2

Three-Point Field Goals: 1979-80, 7-for-31 (.226); 1980-81, 3-for-17 (.176); 1981-82, 6-for-29 (.207); 1982-83, 0-for-21; 1983-84, 6-for-29 (.207); 1984-85, 7-for-37 (.189). Totals: 29-for-164 (.177).

LARRY BIRD

Indiana State University Record

Year	G.	Min.	FGA	FGM	Pct.	FTA	FTM	Pct.	Reb.	Pts.	Avg.
75-76..............				Did Not Play—Transfer Student							
76-77..............	28	1033	689	375	.544	200	168	.840	373	918	32.8
77-78..............	32	....	769	403	.524	193	153	.793	369	950	30.0
78-79..............	34	....	707	376	.532	266	221	.831	505	973	28.6
Totals..............	94	....	2165	1154	.533	659	542	.822	1247	2850	30.3

NBA Regular Season Record

Season—Team	G.	Min.	FGA	FGM	Pct.	FTA	FTM	Pct.	Ast.	PF	Dq.	Stl.	Blk.	Pts.	Avg.
79-80—Boston	82	2955	1463	693	.474	360	301	.836	370	279	4	143	53	1745	21.3
80-81—Boston	82	3239	1503	719	.478	328	283	.863	451	239	2	161	63	1741	21.2
81-82—Boston	77	2923	1414	711	.503	380	328	.863	447	244	0	143	66	1761	22.9
82-83—Boston	79	2982	1481	747	.504	418	351	.840	458	197	0	148	71	1867	23.6
83-84—Boston	79	3028	1542	758	.492	421	374	.888	520	197	0	144	69	1908	24.2
84-85—Boston	80	3161	1760	918	.522	457	403	.882	531	208	0	129	98	2295	28.7
Totals.............	479	18288	9163	4546	.496	2364	2040	.863	2777	1364	6	868	420	11317	23.6

Three-Point Field Goals: 1979-80, 58-for-143 (.406); 1980-81, 20-for-74 (.270); 1981-82, 11-for-52 (.212); 1982-83, 22-for-77 (.286); 1983-84, 18-for-73 (.247); 1984-85, 56-for-131 (.427). *Totals*: 185-for-550 (.336).